101 WAYS TO
FINANCIAL FITNESS

James T. White

Bloomington, IN Milton Keynes, UK

authorHOUSE®

AuthorHouse™
1663 Liberty Drive, Suite 200
Bloomington, IN 47403
www.authorhouse.com
Phone: 1-800-839-8640

AuthorHouse™ UK Ltd.
500 Avebury Boulevard
Central Milton Keynes, MK9 2BE
www.authorhouse.co.uk
Phone: 08001974150

ISBN: 978-1-4343-0552-7 (sc)

Printed in the United States of America
Bloomington, Indiana
This book is printed on acid-free paper.

Library of Congress Control Number: 2007902721

This book is a basic guide only and is not intended to be a replacement for professional advice. Always seek the assistance of a qualified professional before proceeding. Current tax law and local regulations are outside the conditions described in this book. Although specific numbers may have been accurate at the time this book was written, laws may have changed. This book is for entertainment and educational purposes only and does not accept responsibility for the financial conditions of its readers.

Dedication

To my mother and father, my brother Jeffrey, and all my friends. Your support and encouragement has made everything I do possible. Thank you. Also a special thank you to Dale Anderson who helped me put my thoughts on paper.

James T. White

Contents

Chapter Four

DEBT/LOANS: How to Stop Digging When Living in the Hole 22

Chapter Five
BUDGETING: How to, What if, and What Now   27

Chapter Six
INCREASING EARNING POTENTIAL:
Why Make Some When You Can Make More?   34

Chapter Seven
CUTTING COSTS:
Easy Saving Tips That You Can Use on a Daily Basis   **44**

Chapter Eight
IDENTITY THEFT:
Signposts to Watch for on the Information Highway   **55**

Hello and congratulations on beginning your journey to better finances. By reading this book you've already taken your first steps towards educating yourself on becoming a financially fit person.

If you are serious about increasing your earning potential, understanding how your finances work (and don't work) is fundamental in creating capital. It's essential to know what's in your best interests no matter what, and invest accordingly. Basically, becoming wealthy always comes down to individual choices. Rarely do millionaires make one smart business decision and automatically turn into big tycoons. It's a day-to-day mentality of how you want to live your life. It's also a matter of smart, consistent investing, wise planning and dedication. A person with a little extra cash may buy an expensive television, whereas a wannabe millionaire would invest it to turn that little extra cash into a lot of extra cash. By paying attention and working hard, turning from a *thousandaire* to a millionaire may be easier than you thought.

Born and raised in Calgary, Alberta, I was raised to believe in the power of people above all else. My family did not start out rich by any means. We were a lower middle class family struggling like many other families to make ends meet. At four years old I remember my mother dividing one can of tomato soup to feed four people. Seeing that struggle inspired me to work as hard as I could to support myself along with my family. I cannot express the contentment I feel when I am able to take care of my own family, as a thank you for everything they've done for me.

I am not your average 22 year old. I have spent almost my entire life learning, growing, and proving people wrong in business. Everybody has challenges when it comes to being successful and I had to overcome the stereotype associated with my youth. But now I am able to use it as a marketing tool. How many people my age have accomplished what I have? Certainly not many and that's why people trust me. I must know what I'm doing. In fact I have been building successful businesses for over a decade.

It began when I peered outside my window and noticed a person shovelling snow. Immediately the idea for a lawn care business hit me, just like that! In Calgary there will always be snow that needs to be shovelled, and there will always be grass that needs to be cut. Taking this basic supply and demand approach and arming myself with a $20 shovel, I started my first landscaping business at the age of 12 and began networking around my neighbourhood, giving people the opportunity to meet me. I was getting to know the world of business development.

The trick when you are building on an idea is the growth-off-growth approach. I spent the first few years of my landscaping business putting everything I made back into the company, making it more professional. By the time I was fifteen I had invested enough money to afford large industrial equipment like heavy-duty trucks and bobcats, which meant I could offer more advanced landscaping services. The higher the level of service, the higher premium you can charge. This business was fantastic for networking. I dealt with people all the time, making a name for myself. Through one of my clients, I was introduced to the property management business, buying and selling condominiums. This soon became my second company, J & W Property and Asset Management. As time went by, more opportunities became apparent and I continued to build what is now a multi-million dollar enterprise I call J & W Corporate (www.jwcorporate.com). It encompasses my five companies: J&W Mechanical Fleet Services, J&W Lawn Care and Snow Removal, J&W Tire Trax Inc., Courier and Delivery Service, and J&W Property and Asset Management. Currently I am focusing on my newest business, Canam Credit Company Inc., which has already turned into a multi-million dollar international enterprise. There is always a demand for alternative money solutions, especially in a big city like Calgary, and this company responds to these needs by providing business factoring and private lending.

Whether you live in a small town or big city, or hold small or large account balances, there is always space to grow and that's what I love about the financial world. Living in Calgary during an economic boom not seen since the oil growth in the 1970's has been an exciting and prosperous time and has taught me a lot about the business world. The trick to making money anywhere is taking advantage of every opportunity and never giving up. If you're smart and more importantly, AWARE, then moneymaking possibilities start opening up everywhere. The key lies in networking. The more networking you can do, the more your name gets out there and the more people think of you when opportunity comes along. For this reason, never forget a name! Write it down, include it in your roll-a-dex or add it to your Christmas card list. Do whatever you have to in keeping that contact because you never know where it could lead! Never assume anything about a person you meet for the first time. By judging someone you could automatically be shutting a door to a chance in make lots of money. Whether the person is a customer in your business or a stranger at a party there could be an opportunity. You just need to create it.

For some reason people think that to be financially successful you have to give up the things you love: entertainment, time, relationships, morals, etc. It's just not true. Certainly a person's focus may change, but it's about finding new passions and discovering new possibilities. What's important is being creative and different when it comes to business and money, and that involves changing, even creating markets where you see a demand or opportunity.

Ever heard the expression, money makes the world go round? Well it's not 100% untrue. Think about how many times you use, think about and discuss money every day. Now think about all the areas in the financial world that you don't understand or wish to understand better. Instead of trying to grasp overwhelming financial concepts, how about taking practical advice that you can incorporate into your everyday life? I promise you will learn something in this book, something you can use to increase your earning potential and preserve the money you already have. It doesn't have to be as complicated as you might think. No matter what age, location or tax bracket you happen to be in, your money has the potential to grow in ways you may not even realize.

Now I don't want to make it seem like becoming rich is easy, it isn't. It takes hard work, a smart business sense and many, many x-factors. But by becoming knowledgeable on the markets and by networking, you can eliminate many of these x-factors and start making smarter choices when it comes to your money. The best way to do that is by gaining access to information that will help your money grow. If you are well aware of your financial situation and are willing to learn more about the financial world around you, it's amazing how many opportunities start appearing seemingly out of nowhere.

Money cannot make your dreams come true, but it can make it a lot easier to create opportunities for those dreams to become reality. The rest is up to you and what you are willing to do to make yourself as happy as you can be in life. Success is a completely relative term, the important thing is to set goals and live up to all of your own expectations. That's how you get ahead in the world and make it easier to live life on your terms.

I truly hope you gain the financial prosperity you are searching for and can incorporate the things you learn in this book into your daily life. Good luck on your pursuit and think of me when you buy your first mansion, sports car, or take your dream vacation!

Sincerely,

James T. White

Chapter One

STOCK/INVESTMENTS: Spread the Wealth

Benjamin Franklin once said, "An investment in knowledge always pays the best interest", well old Ben certainly knew what he was talking about. The trick to investing properly (and profitably) is in understanding the market and making reasonable choices based on your risk tolerance. That may sound easy enough, but it's usually in the details where most people get lost. There is a lot of money to be made in the stock market, so it's important that you understand just how much money you can make and potentially lose while playing the investment game.

1. What is a *stock* in a company?

A stock is an investment in a company that sells shares of that company in order to free up money for expansions and improvements, and of course financial gain. When you own stock you are *shareholder* and you own a part of that company, in which each share of that stock is worth a certain price. This price then changes depending on how successful the company is (or often how well it is *perceived* to be doing). So if you buy stock at ten dollars a share, and a year later the company has grown and offers to sell stock at twenty dollars, you are doing very well as a stockholder. (Keep in mind you have to sell your stock to see any actual money.)

Stocks do not offer guarantees, so be careful when choosing which stocks to invest in. You can buy stock in a private company or a publicly traded company that is listed on a stock exchange such as the TSX, Venture, or Dow Jones Industrial Average (DJIA). Typically you must be an accredited investor if you are interested in a private company, which means you represent a bank or a trust, are a director or executive, or are worth a lot of money (anything above and beyond 200,000 dollars) in most cases.

2. I want to invest my money in something. What do I look for before I start?

Investments can be a daunting and intimidating task, especially if you've never invested before. Make sure you are in a financially smart position before you begin; you do not want to be nose-deep in credit card debt or living paycheck to paycheck while throwing money into stock. Next consider your choices of long-term investments. Consider your goals when doing this (child's education, retirement, etc.). This will give you a better understanding of the amount of time the investment will have to grow. Choosing an investment is a tricky process, so meet with an investment broker whom you are sure has your best interest in mind. Some do not work with new or small accounts. Try spreading your investments around to reduce risk. That way if your stock is low, your bonds may be high. Speaking of risk, if you are a beginner investor, try mutual funds. They can be low risk and diversify your portfolio.

Whatever you invest in, make sure you fully understand the ins and outs of the process. You will inevitably be more successful as an investor if you feel confident in the people you are investing in. Make sure you understand the short- and long-term goals of the company and whether it can be successful in its business. This takes education and guesswork, so tread carefully.

3. My good friend told me to invest in something I've never heard of. But he swears it is a guarantee. Should I invest?

It's your money, so only invest in something you are comfortable with. The market is dependant on so many variables that NOTHING IS A GUARANTEE. So do some research; if you feel the management of the company can succeed in both slow and fast times, then invest. Especially when dealing with smaller companies, it always comes down to the person you're investing in. You can have a great idea and the person in charge can ruin it, whereas a good leader can make a success out of anything.

No matter what, focus on what's on paper and what your gut says, not on what somebody else is telling you.

4. Is there any way to predict how the stock market will shift?

The best way to "predict the future" and make money is to buy shares at a very low price, private placements for example, and sell high when the company goes IPO (goes public). This is how you make real cash and stay away from the blue-chip stock. If you are curious about what factors drive certain sectors of the stock market, there are several books and articles on stock market theory. Mainly you have to look at the macroeconomics. This includes government decisions, international factors, and entry and exit of well-known investors into certain sectors. The U.S. stock market contains about 60 percent of the world's economy, which would make the New York Stock Exchange (NYSE) a major influence. An easy way (using the term loosely) to research a sector is by accessing a firm's securities research. Otherwise you can access governmental statistics Web sites such as the site of the Federal Reserve or the Office of Management and Budget. Whatever you do, remember that the stock market will always be unpredictable since natural disasters and world tragedies will always affect how people spend money, so play with caution.

5. Are there ways to safely practice investing in the stock market?

A fun way to gain necessary market knowledge is to access a Web site that offers a simulation of the stock market, giving you play money, with which you can practice for free. This is not only a safe way to get to know the market for those who have no clue how it works, it also can be fun to invest tons of money that you don't have just to see what happens. The site also can assist sophisticated investors looking to test out advanced strategies. These sites have a system that connects to a real-life data feed and can support trading in North American exchanges, option trading, and short selling, and adjusts for most corporate actions such as mergers and dividends. So get online, have fun, and become a virtual millionaire (or a virtual bum)!

6. How do I begin to "play" in the stock market?

Before investing your hard-earned dollars, a key recommendation would definitely be to *educate yourself.* Knowledge will get you much further than luck when it comes to the stock market. Many factors determine where people invest their money: news reports, world events, astrology, because the dog barked at the T.V. when a stock appeared, etc. Just how you invest is ultimately up to you; however, to begin effectively, learn how the best traders are buying and selling and why. You can do this on the stock simulator on free websites, or do your own research with top traders that you know, in person or in books. In case these top traders are tight-lipped in terms of their investments (You can't blame them.), you can always model your trading on somebody who is very successful. Of course, there are no guarantees, but it might give you a better idea of how the game is played. Nothing beats experience, so either imitate somebody else's or get your own.

7. What should I look for in insurance companies?

Do not put your life in the wrong hands! When shopping for any kind of insurance, you should always consider the firm's financial condition. It is important that the company you choose can and will pay your claim. Secondly, you need to have a good knowledge of your insurance needs. This will depend on your specific situation. Lastly, it will serve you well to shop around for the best rate for what you need. An easy way to do this would be surfing the Web (Some Web sites even provide a price comparison.) or by calling companies asking for rate information.

8. What is the difference between registered and non-registered funds?

Registered funds protect your investments and their earnings from tax, whereas unregistered funds do not. Typically, a registered fund is used for long-term investments, such as a child's education or retirement. A non-registered fund may be more fitting for short-term investments, like saving for a car or a vacation.

9. What are the advantages and disadvantages to mutual funds?

This is like asking how many raindrops are in a cloud. The sector exploded in the 1990s, and now there are currently over 80 million Americans that invest in mutual funds, and the industry is worth over 400 billion dollars in Canada. A mutual fund is a company that raises money by selling shares to its investors. In return for purchasing shares, investors receive a proportional share in the pool of fund assets. There is a range in degrees of diversification between mutual funds. Generally, one advantage to a mutual fund investment is that it gives small investors access to a well-diversified portfolio of securities such as equities and bonds. Another advantage to mutual funds is liquidity. Shares can be bought and sold by the shareholder and can be accessed whenever necessary. Mutual fund investments typically fail to beat the market, however, and it is difficult to pick a fund that has a better chance to do well. That is to say, past performance has little influence on future standings. When selling your mutual fund, be aware of tax consequences and back-end loads (charges that affect your total redemption value). A fund manager invests your money based on market conditions in order to reach specified objectives that are in the original prospectus. Deciding which mutual fund to invest in and with what company is up to you, but due diligence will certainly serve you well in this case.

Chapter Two

REAL ESTATE: Making Sense Out of Property

Property ownership is big business. Whether you're buying, selling, renting, or flipping, your home can provide the security you need beyond lock and key.

Real estate runs a different track from other financial ventures because it's a market that most people are involved with one way or the other. If you're smart in your real estate choices and aware of what's going on, you could end up richer than you ever thought possible. Keep in mind that the real estate market is very much reliant on where you are living, so independent research is always necessary.

1. Real estate is a safe investment, isn't it?

Safe is a complicated word when it comes to investments. The real estate market is so dependant on the national economy and so many other variables that it can fluctuate up or down. Generally, you will not pay the full price of your real estate investment but a fraction of it. Any growth the investment may see would apply to that initial principle. This way you can pay, say $15,000 for a $150,000 house and any rate increases on that investment will be taken off the $15,000. So even if the house value goes up 3 or 4 percent, it still may be a significant return on your small investment. For short-term profit, I would say invest in something other than real estate because you have to worry about property maintenance and this could get costly. This being said, real estate is also a good investment in that it opens up doors that were previously closed to you. If you own your own home, you are more easily approved for credit and obviously pay a mortgage rather than rent, which is a steadier payment.

2. Is it profitable to sublet your home?

Subletting can be a lucrative move, if you are able to pull it off and are willing to put up with the consequences. Firstly you should be sure that you are *allowed* to sublet. Some landlords prefer you not to. Also, be aware of how much you are charging. There can be legal ramifications to asking for more rent than you actually pay. (You could be sued!) You can find a lawyer who specializes in real estate to help you with the legal side of things. On the plus side, subletting your home can be profitable when you are living outside the area for an extended period of time. Just make sure the tenant you sublet to is dependable. As well, avoid setting up an illegal basement suite. Though these are everywhere in large cities, you could get into some big trouble if you are found out.

3. What is house flipping? How much money can you make?

House flipping is the process of buying a piece of real estate at a relatively low cost, improving the quality of the property, and selling it at a heightened cost in a quick amount of time. Necessary for the process to work is an interested investor, a talented and ambitious home renovator (or team of renovators), and the determination to carry it through. Many investors use family and friends as renovators. There is definitely the potential to make a lot of money in a short amount of time, but there are consequences. Sometimes work is done too fast and the quality of the work suffers. That is why usually more than one appraisal on the house should be done before selling. Many people make full-time careers out of house flipping and dedicate hundreds of hours of remodelling to realize a profit on their investment. There is no guarantee, however, that the price you sell the property for will match or exceed the money you put into fixing it up.

4. What are the benefits of owning a home over renting?

Most people dream of owning a home, and with this dream come benefits when compared to those who rent. As the value of the house rises over time, owners build equity and enjoy shrinking mortgage balances. Also, owners do not have to worry about housing costs skyrocketing because unless borrowers have adjustable-rate mortgages, lenders cannot increase rates and payments. As a renter, your rent payments may increase many times without consent. By owning a home, you are investing in more than just real estate; you are investing in your future. So be smart and plan ahead!

5. What are the downsides to owning rather than renting?

With ownership comes responsibility and lots of it! There is no landlord to complain to when the pipes break or when the furnace is shot. It's all up to you to fix. This is why it's usually not a good idea to throw all your money into a huge down-payment, because you'll need a little extra cash in case something happens. It is also very important that buyers understand where they stand in terms of job security. You do not want to be a new homeowner and newly unemployed! Payments can also add up unexpectedly and must be kept in mind. Buyers are required to pay closing costs and other home-buying fees, along with the commission to the real estate agent—not to mention the monthly payments! As a renter, the move-in costs are cheaper, usually a damage deposit and a security deposit, which may or may not be returned to you when you move out.

6. What should my monthly mortgage payment be in relation to my monthly net income?

Lenders and banks vary in their calculations for what is acceptable. Some lenders want your total ratio to be less than 36 percent for your home and 45 percent of your total debt. Some, however, allow up to 80 percent debt-to-income ratio to approve a mortgage loan. It all depends on your situation and the willingness of your mortgage broker to give you a loan. Keep in mind that these payments can be refinanced later (fixed to adjustable rates) to accommodate your changing financial circumstances.

7. What is better: a home equity loan or a second mortgage?

Really this depends on what you intend to do. A home equity loan is basically a line of credit and can be paid whenever you like. Most of the time there are no closing costs. A second mortgage is a second lien on your house and issued as a one-time, lump-sum amount that can be borrowed on either a fixed or variable rate of interest. Home equity loans have more flexibility and typically cost less, but a second mortgage may help if you only need to borrow money for one occasion, say to pay for a large investment. Just like any other loan, factors you should consider would be your income and risk tolerance.

8. How do I find out the value of my home? Is it important to know even if I'm not selling my home?

To know the value of your home is to know how much leverage you have in the financial world. To a creditor, a wink and a smile will only get you so far, whereas equity will get you much further. It is important to know the value of your estate because many business loans and other kinds of loans are secured against real estate, meaning that agencies will lend you money only if you own property. (This protects them from refusal or lack of repayment.) The best way to assess the value of your home is to hire a certified appraiser to assess your house. Usually the homeowner is responsible for this payment, but many times residential appraisers agree to accept orders from lending institutions with the understanding that payment will be made following settlement or closing of the loan.

9. What do I do when looking for a real estate agent?

Searching for a real estate agent can be tricky business. If you know what to look for, you could be saving yourself from trouble. In any industry, *experience* is almost always an asset, but it is of particular importance in the real estate industry. Ask your agent how many sales they close a year, how many years they've conducted business, and what kind of training was necessary. You have a right to know this, and if your agent is a professional, he or she should have no problem answering your questions. Further, there is no replacing good ol' *skill*. You need to know your agent can perform his or her duties confidently and wisely. Does your agent have intimate awareness of technical aspects of contracts such as negotiations, inspections, and appraisals? Most real estate agents have *market knowledge* of a specific area in which they generally operate their business. An agent who specializes in the west end of the city may not be helpful when selling on the east end. By knowing the community in which you are buying or selling, the agent will be aware of comparable prices and what has happened, what is currently happening, and what is going to happen in the area. Keep in mind your agent must work *for you*. The agent must have a proper *work ethic* and make an effort to work around your schedule, which includes evenings and weekends, to show your home. (This is when most buyers and sellers are available.) Agents should always be easy to contact and not bogged down with other business. Remember, you are the priority! Find an agent with *integrity*. You cannot put a price on honesty. Buying or selling your home is too big of a deal to have a sleaze as an agent, so make sure he or she is looking out for your best interests and not looking to make a quick buck. Lastly, *resources* are valuable assets in the business of real estate. Agents may have convenient Web site access to home listings and good relationships with mortgage brokers that could help you out. Any resource can be an advantage and will make you a buck or two!

10. How can I estimate moving costs?

Moving your belongings from your house can be a stressful and expensive chore. But unless you want to give up all of your possessions, it's pretty much necessary. Make sure to plan ahead in order to get an idea of how much you're willing to spend. If you are using a moving company, call ahead and talk to a representative. Let them know the square footage of your home as well as any large pieces of furniture you own, and ask about any and all costs that are involved in the move. They should be able to give a rough estimate based on the number of boxes and materials needed. There is also typically a price chart showing the distance the moving vehicle must travel.

If you decide to move on your own, decide what size truck you need, or better yet, get a friend who owns a truck. (If you don't have a friend, GET ONE!) Also consider what materials you will need (boxes, tape, etc.) and if you'll need to hire additional help for sensitive furniture or to clean your home once it's cleaned out. Planning your moving budget prior to moving may open up some room to reduce costs, but more importantly it will make a normally stressful day a little less stressful!

Chapter Three

Credit and You:
Welcome to the Wonderful World of Credit

Credit can be a great thing or something to be feared, depending on your attitude. If you don't understand how credit works but use it anyway, you could be taking a lot of unnecessary risks without many rewards. If you tend to get caught up in the plastic world of credit and debit cards, then smarten up! This is dangerous for you and WILL NOT HELP YOU! For many in this world of convenience, credit can be just a little too convenient.

If you treat credit responsibly and know how to use it, then you have nothing to worry about. It can benefit you throughout your life and open doors that you may not even realize. The problem most people have is they don't understand the ins and outs of the credit industry and don't know their options. Well, here's your chance. Grab a pen!

1. Which is better: several credit cards with low balances or one credit card with a high balance?

Your credit score could be affected if you hold several credit cards with low balances. This would ultimately affect the percentage rates you are charged when you apply for loans. When banks see you with several credit cards, it sends them a message that you may be desperate for credit, making you a risk. It is best to keep one credit card with a high balance. (You can always try to bargain with the credit companies to lower your monthly interest payment.)

2. What should I do with my credit card receipts?

The Canada Customs and Revenue Agency has the right to review up to seven years of financial data if they conduct an audit on you. For this reason, it is a good idea to keep a file that holds all of your receipts going back seven years. Keeping these credit card transactions and other receipts may save you time, stress, and cost later on. As well, having all of your receipts in one place will help you if there are any mistakes on your statement, if you have to refer back to them during tax time, or when reviewing your budget.

3. When trying to get approved, should I apply for as many credit cards as possible?

Although this practice may be tempting, avoid it, as it actually *decreases* your chances of getting approved. For one thing, creditors will look at your total unused credit line on all of your cards. If you have the ability to charge $40,000 on your credit cards but in fact only owe around $1,000, a potential creditor may look to the $40,000 spending power as if you already owed that money. Also, when you apply for credit the issuer requests a copy of your credit report, which shows up as an inquiry on your report. Since creditors assume that many of the inquiries on your report have resulted in credit being granted, they may refuse to extend more credit to you based on this assumption.

4. What is the best way to lower my credit card interest rates?

If your credit card payments are too high, debt consolidation may be for you and won't impair your credit profile. Consolidating your debt can also help you by improving your credit rating, and the interest is tax deductible which helps your total savings. Keep in mind that not all debt consolidation runs the same track. The process depends on whether you own or rent your home, your monthly income-to-debt ratio, and your current credit rating. A less time-consuming option is to call your credit company and tell them you're credit shopping and you will not pay their high rates. They want to keep your business and will many times lower the rate. If the representative declines your request, ask to speak to the credit manager and keep climbing the chain of command. I guarantee you will save money. In addition to doing this with interest rates, ask them to waive your annual fee. Chances are they will if you put a little effort into it.

5. What role do credit bureaus play in an individual receiving credit?

Credit bureaus are the gatekeepers to the wonderful land of credit. There are approximately 1,297 credit bureaus and caisses populaires in Canada. These bureaus gather information on how you use credit and reveal to the potential lenders your credit history, which essentially explains whether or not you are a credit risk. The lender decides from the credit report if you are able and willing to repay the credit. There are three major bureaus in Canada: Equifax

Canada, NCB Inc., and TransUnion Canada. In the United States, they are Equifax, Experian, and TransUnion.

6. How does a creditor decide if you're creditworthy?

By knowing how a creditor will evaluate you, not only is the mystery removed from the process, more importantly, you can take major steps toward improving your credit profile and increasing your chances of getting your credit approved. When you apply for credit by filling out an application, the form typically gives the creditor permission to retrieve your credit report from a credit bureau. Once this is done, the creditor assesses your credit worthiness based on both objective and subjective criteria.

Many lending institutions will employ a short-term debt-to-income ratio with which they calculate your present short-term debt payments and divide it by your total annual income. Generally creditors will not lend to you if your short-term debt is more than 20 percent of your annual income. Similarly, a potential creditor will add up all your monthly bills (not including rent/mortgage and utilities) and divide by your gross income. Here, creditors are looking for a ratio of under 35 percent. It is a good idea to look through your credit report and find the credit card accounts that you no longer want and cancel them.

Most lending institutions employ their own version of a credit worthiness scoring system with which they assess your credit information. The number of years at your job tells creditors about your level of consistency, and the kind of work you do holds importance as well. Manual work is seen as being less favorable than clerical work. Next preferred is whether you are self-employed, managerial, and most favored is the almighty professional. This preference is based mainly on job stability.

The number and nature of the blotches on your credit history also send up red flags, the worst of course being bankruptcy. Creditors also look at the amount of credit you currently have. How much debt could you go into if you maxed out your present cards? Finally, creditors also look at whether you have a telephone in your own name, the length of time you have been at your present address and whether you own your home.

7. What is a credit score? Why is it important?

A credit score is a number based on your credit history that potential lenders use to assess whether or not to give you credit. The number can range from three hundred to nine hundred(the higher the better) and is calculated based on a number of factors. It considers your payment history (including late payments, collections, bankruptcies, etc.) and your outstanding debt. The more credit you've racked up on your cards, the lower the score will be. The length of time you've had established credit is also evaluated since the more information a lender can assess, the better prediction he or she can make in lending credit. The *types* of credit you currently have are also assessed. This would include the number of loans you have and the types of accounts you hold. Lastly, a high number of inquiries on your report may lower your credit score since it reveals, in a way, how many times you've applied for credit.

The advantage of a credit score is that it makes the process of assessing creditworthiness quick, easy, and objective. The number reveals to the lender immediately how much of a risk you are. Before applying for credit, it may be a good idea to find out your credit score by visiting Web sites that provide the service or by requesting the information when you are applying for a loan.

8. What happens to your credit score when you get married?

Initially, nothing happens. Once you are married, you may, however, decide to apply for credit for a mortgage, car loan, and so on. At this point, if you apply together, your partner's credit will affect the interest rate (assuming you're approved). Whatever happens with that line of credit from that point on affects both your credit scores. (Remember that whole "for richer or for poorer" thing?) If one person has good credit and the other bad, you can consider applying for credit separate from one another.

9. What are the kinds of negative marks that can appear on my credit and how bad are they?

The following is a list of most of the negative items that could appear on your credit report. They are listed in order of what many creditors would consider as best to worst.

Credit inquiries – how many times your report has been requested

Credit rejections – how many times you've been rejected for credit

Late payments – shows your reliability

Past due and unpaid payments – shows your potential to miss future payments

Court judgments – any proceedings that may affect your credit

Collections – assets collected from you due to lack of payment

Loan defaults – you did not pay back the loan or violated conditions of the loan agreement

Repossession – retrieving items purchased in order to pay back the loan

Foreclosure – property that has been foreclosed due to financial instability

Bankruptcy- unable to pay back loan; includes chapter of bankruptcy

10. How long does information stay on my credit report?

Timeframes depend on what information you are referring to. Keep in mind that in given circumstances, for example when you are applying for life insurance that is over $50,000, the credit bureau may supply information that is longer than the allocated timeframes.

Delinquent payments: Even if you later pay off the account in full, payments to your creditors that are made over thirty days past due will remain on your credit report for three to seven years.

Collection accounts: After as little as three months of payment delinquency, a creditor can turn your account over for collections. Your credit report will reflect the collection activity for seven years from the time the first payment you missed was due. If you pay off the account after collection activity has commenced, your credit report will still be marked for seven years but may say "paid collection."

Inquiries: Inquiries are notations in your credit report marking a request to view your credit report. For example, when you fill out an application for a credit card, the credit card company asks the credit bureau for a copy of your credit report, creating an inquiry notation. Most inquiries remain for two years. Note that too many inquires on your credit report can reduce your credit rating.

Charge-offs: These occur when a creditor decides that they would rather write off your debt as a loss than attempt to collect it from you. Such charge-offs remain on your credit for seven years from the time of the first missed payment.

Bankruptcy: Chapter 7, 11, and 12 bankruptcies stay on credit for ten years from the date of filing. Chapter 13 bankruptcies stay on your credit for seven years after the discharge, which is usually three to five years after filing.

11. Does this mean I have to wait seven to ten years before I can get a loan if I have bad credit?

Although negative information stays on your credit report for up to ten years, it is possible to be approved for credit in the meantime. Creditors are much more interested in your present circumstances than what happened to you five or ten years ago. Therefore, rebuilding your credit can be done relatively quickly through a systematic plan and a little perseverance. Keep in mind that positive credit information stays on your credit report indefinitely!

12. What if I'm turned down for credit?

By law the creditor must do two things along with your rejection letter. They must provide you with the specific reasons why you were rejected and give the name and address of the credit bureau used to make the decision. If the reason why you were rejected sounds inaccurate, immediately get a copy of your credit report from the same bureau and analyze it for errors. If you find a mistake, contact the bureau and supply the necessary information to fix it. Afterward reapply to the same creditor, attaching an explanation and an updated copy of your credit report.

If you were rejected based on accurate data, you may still appeal the rejection by sending a letter to the creditor explaining why you are a better credit risk than your credit report may indicate. However, most likely you will have to jump through hoops and meet certain conditions to rebuild your credit before they will approve your application. But hey, what's a little hoop jumping for credit approval?

13. Should I use a credit counselling company to help me settle my debts?

Debt relief is very much a case-by-case circumstance. The key is in understanding exactly where you stand regarding how much you spend, how much you make, and how much you owe. The more information you have, the easier time you'll have getting out of debt. You can do it by yourself, but some credit counselling companies can get a larger debt settlement. They do this by collectively making an offer to a bank to settle much more than just your debt alone. It's less of a headache for you as well. If credit counselling doesn't work for you, you can try debt consolidation, debt negotiation, or as a last resort, bankruptcy.

14. What are the advantages of joining a credit union?

Credit unions offer loans, financial counselling, savings, and other related services. Because credit unions are member-owned and you are a member, you have the power to direct policy. Not only are you able to pool your savings because credit unions are not-for-profit organizations, they operate at a lower cost, assuring good rates on your saving investments and low interest rates on loans. As well, you are entitled to run for the board of directors and attend meetings, which could help networking and teach you more about the financial world.

15. Are debit cards are good method of payment?

Debit card transactions are a *popular* method of payment because it involves spending money that you currently own. It may sound crazy, but if you are financially unhealthy, it's actually a good idea to cut up your debit card altogether! Too many problems arise out of misusing debit cards due to not keeping track of purchases. Without direct access to your funds at all times, you would be surprised by how much money you save! (This also applies to credit cards. There's no sense in spending money you neither have nor will have).

16. Are there charges for using my debit card?

Every person with a debit card has an account with specific information and limitations; some may be limited to, say, sixty transactions a month without charge. If this works for you, great, but if not, beware of making purchases at a small cost for each further transaction. If you were to use your debit card on an ATM that your bank is not affiliated with, there may be an even smaller limit to transactions without charge. It pays to keep track of your card transactions! Moreover, some small businesses charge a couple of dollars for very small purchases on your debit card, say, if you're spending two dollars or less. If they do charge a fee, they must post a sign saying so. To learn more about your personal limits and exceptions, contact your bank.

17. What happens if my debit card is stolen? Am I liable for any false charges?

The first thing you should do as soon as you lose your debit card is report it to your bank and file a police report. The sooner you do this, the better. Most banks cover anything over fifty dollars in charges, and some will cover the entire cost, provided you report the card missing immediately.

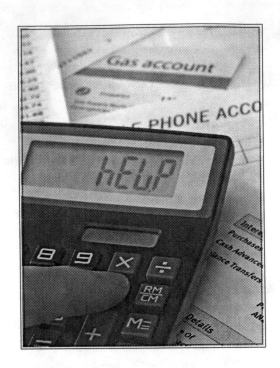

Chapter Four

DEBT/LOANS:
How to Stop Digging When Living in the Hole

Most people live in debt. This doesn't have to be a huge problem in your life, as long as it is kept under control and steps are constantly being taken to lessen the gap between you and financial independence. Debt and lending can be a scary path to take for most people, but it is the dedication to long- and short-term goals that makes the difference when entering into and exiting out of the pitfalls of debt. Remember to be smart when thinking about your debt situation. Consider how it affects your life, what steps you will take to alleviate the stresses that debt and loans usually bring with them, and you may discover that the situation may not be as grim and scary as you made it out to seem. A little perseverance and knowledge could end up saving you tons of dough.

1. Is it better to save money or pay off debt?

Without a doubt, paying off any debt is more beneficial to you because the interest you pay on debt is much greater than the interest you earn while saving money. Psychologically speaking as well, being debt-free will help you sleep better.

2. Should I consolidate my debt with a second mortgage?

A second mortgage loan may lower your payments by consolidating your debt. However, you must be aware of the costs. You are required to put your home up for collateral, so if you don't keep up the payments, you may not keep your home. However, remember that home equity loans may provide you with tax advantages that you would not find in other kinds of loans.

3. How long does it take from the time a credit card debt is past due until they turn it over to collections?

It can vary, but the general rule is anywhere between three months and seven months. Keep in mind there is statute of limitations for how long the creditor or collection agency can hassle for your money, depending on where you live. Remember, if you let a large balance go unpaid for a long period of time, your credit score will end up being very low and will hurt your chances of any future loan approvals.

4. What are the pros and cons of bankruptcy?

Bankruptcy occurs when a person in debt can no longer provide the necessary payments and creditors are unwilling to provide more credit or restructure the debt. Of course, bankruptcy should always be considered the last resort. It is a hard road to travel in achieving a financial solution, but it will get you there legally and gives you a chance at future stability.

The positives of bankruptcy are fairly clear. It enables you to legally take care of your debt, protects you from hounding creditors, and essentially gives you a fresh financial start. However, this does not come without a cost. You will still have to go to court, and you may lose your assets. (You typically keep basic household goods, depending on what province or state you live in.)

5. What is the difference between a fixed rate and an adjustable rate? Which one is better?

An adjustable rate *adjusts* over time depending on how the loan was set up, whereas a fixed rate is a constant rate over the life of the loan. What is best depends on the economic climate; lately a fixed rate has been better because it isn't affected by fluctuations in interest rates over the course of the loan. For example, if you have a 4 percent loan at a fixed rate for twenty years, it means you only pay 4 percent on the loan for 20 years. An adjustable rate varies either up or down based on the interest rate, typically every five years. If the interest rate increases to 10 percent, this is what you will be paying for that period of the loan. (Keep in mind interest rates could lower as well.) Exactly which rate is better really depends on whether you are dealing with a rising-rate system (wherein fixed rates would win out by staying low) or a low-rate system, whereby an adjustable rate would be preferable. It is difficult to determine which of these two environments we will see in the next few years because past performance is no indicator.

6. I need money fast. Is borrowing from friends and family a good idea?

This depends on your family and friends. Generally, your support system is a good place to go when you need any kind of help, and if your friends and family know you well enough, they will decide for themselves whether you are worth the risk of lending money. Many times these people will forgo interest payments, which can save you money. However, lending from family and friends can end up getting ugly and ruining relationships. Too many of these cases end up in small-claims court, so tread lightly and act responsibly.

There are a few pointers that you should keep in mind to protect the situation from getting emotional. *Step one:* DON'T GET EMOTIONAL! Leave your financial agreements out of any other squabble or argument you may have. *Step Two:* Get everything in writing. People, no matter how good their intentions are, are fallible. Getting all the details and numbers down on paper protects everybody from forgetfulness or disagreements. This helps the process go smoothly, especially if the relationship ends during the repayment process. *Step Three:* Decide on an official plan of repayment, including a completion date. *Step Four:* Pay the person back! You do not want to be "that friend" whom nobody loans money to; that person usually ends up lonely and poor.

7. My friend/family member asked me for a loan, but he/she doesn't have the greatest history with money. What can I do to ensure I get my money back?

When lending money to a person who is close to you, treat the process just as if you were lending to a stranger. This helps things from getting emotional and protects you from being taken advantage of. Since you do not have the luxury of directly withdrawing money from the person's bank account, you have to depend on him or her to pay you. If you are not sure whether the person can do that, reconsider the loan. Or you can help protect your position by setting up a contract with the person stating all the details of the lending agreement, including a repayment schedule and any interest rates, and having each party understand it, agree to it, and sign it. The process of repayment can be flexible, making a payment every week, bi-monthly, monthly, etc. Whatever it is, make sure it is realistic in order to avoid problems! Remember, you are the banker in this situation, so be strong and do not let your friend or family member weasel out of anything! If both parties are responsible and respectful, the process will go off without a hitch and you will feel great for helping out a friend in need.

8. What should I know before I co-sign a loan?

As a co-signer, you are basically lending somebody good enough credit to obtain a loan or become approved for something financially. If the person you co-sign for begins to miss payments, the creditors come after you and you are held accountable for the money. This is why you should always be very cautious when thinking about co-signing anything and make sure you back yourself up financially. Say you're co-signing a loan for property. If you are not sure the person is financially stable enough, you might consider buying the property yourself and renting it to them until they can afford to buy. Or why not split the payments for the property? That way if the signer does not come through with the payments, you at least have some ownership rights. Whatever the situation, the most important thing to remember is whether or not the person you are co-signing for is credible to you. Assess the risk honestly. Everybody makes mistakes in their past and many have streaks of bad luck, but beyond that you don't want to mess with your credit without having done anything. Ask yourself how long you have known this person. Do you think you'll know him or her two years from now? Whatever you do, don't co-sign something just to be nice.

9. I just received a hefty inheritance. What should I do with the money?

Depending on the amount of the inheritance, there are some smart ways to invest your money and make some long-term plans. Assuming it is a large inheritance, setting up an emergency fund (upwards to $10,000) is a great start. You could increase your 401(k) contribution and put some aside for your child's education. Your mortgage: to pay or not to pay? The answer depends on the interest rate you're paying. If it's low, you can probably find a better investment that could give you a higher return. Otherwise, pay it off instead of having your money sit in a savings account with a very low interest rate.

Chapter Five

BUDGETING: How to, What if, and What Now

In order to ever be financially successful, you need to fully understand every aspect of your money: where it comes from, where it goes, and most importantly, how you can reduce unnecessary costs. This does not have to be a difficult task. Usually it is simply a matter of a little homework, diligence, and commitment. Coming up with some kind of plan will help you in the short term and long term.

1. How do I make a personal financial plan?

Personal planning is a smart, relatively easy way to ensure (or at least increase the chances) of financial stability and progress. It is different from a budget because it can be much more vague. It is not an action but an overview of your financial situation and doesn't set strict rules or limitations. It involves understanding your net worth, setting financial goals, and working out a basic plan to achieve them. Sound easy? It can be, but it's usually not a quick process. Begin by writing down all of your financial goals. Break each one of these down into several short-term, medium-term, and long-term goals. Where do you see yourself in five years? How about twenty years? Next become educated on ways to sustain and develop these areas of your finances. This may take some time and require some reading but will pay off in the end. Evaluating your progress is essential and will show you whether or not it is working. Remember that following a successful financial plan means being realistic and making smart money choices on a daily basis. It involves being committed and disciplined. Another obstacle to smart financial planning is procrastination. So start NOW! There is no time like the present to become financially healthy!

2. How important is a budget?

A business cannot function without a budget and neither should you. A budget lets you control your money instead of your money controlling you. It will tell you whether or not you are living within your means and help you focus on important goals. Additionally, knowing exactly where your money is and where it is going will give you a better perspective of which direction you're heading in financially. A budget can get you out of debt and keep you there by revealing aspects of your spending that are either unnecessary or inflated, which in turn will help you sleep better at night. Also, sticking to a budget will actually free up some extra cash to save, invest, or treat yourself to something special. It will also reserve funds for any emergency or unforeseen expenses that may (and probably will) pop up.

3. What should my budget include?

Start by putting on paper how much you make, how much you spend, and how much you owe. This will give you a good overview of your financial situation and help predict any future complications. Include any possible financial burdens that are not planned but could happen in the next year or so. This could include losing your job if you have low job security, health complications, a possible move, etc. Next write down specific financial goals you have. Do you want to start saving for your child's education? What about a new car or a vacation getaway? A budget will help you get there and will help you stay motivated.

Keep receipts! Have a place in your home to place all credit card, gas, and food receipts, and add them up at the end of each month. If you are spending too much on food, for example, try cooking at home more often. Next consider your outstanding debt and stick to a repayment plan. Mortgages, car loans, and business loans should all be included. Lastly and most importantly, make your budget realistic. Life is hard and there is no sense in making it harder by living up to your own crazy expectations. If you work out a plan you can stick to, you are more likely to follow through with it in the long run. Good luck.

4. How do I figure out my net worth?

Knowing your net worth is important for anyone who wants to be financially stable. No matter what your situation, figuring out where you are standing financially will benefit you by giving you more control over where your money goes and will help you when applying for a mortgage, credit card, car loan, or any other financial aid. Your net worth is the difference between your *assets* (the things you own) and your *liabilities* (the things you owe). The goal is simply to have more assets than liabilities. To figure this out, get a piece of paper, a pen, and your thinking cap. Write down the value of everything that you own, including cash (or cash equivalents), investments, real estate, household goods, retirement funds, etc. Total the value of these assets. Next list off all of your liabilities. These can include any loans, mortgages, credit card balances, and taxes. Total the value of this list. Now subtract your liabilities from your assets. If you have a positive number, you are doing great! If the number is negative, now is the time to figure out what to do to change your financial situation. Something to keep in mind when figuring out your net worth is that you must include every miscellaneous item or investment that is worth money. Everyone will have a different list, but if you are not sure, it is best to use a net-worth sample worksheet, available online or at your bank, as a checklist.

5. What are some easy ways to put aside money on a daily basis?

Believe it or not, there are some easy ways to save money every day that may not seem significant at first but can and will add up eventually. When you get home from work, school, errands, wherever, put the spare change from your pocket into a jar stashed somewhere where you will always see it. It may take awhile to add up, but the benefits can be substantial and help you out when you need it.

Are you always being told to control your bad language? Contain that loose tongue by starting a swear jar. A quarter or a dollar owed for each bad word will add up and save you from embarrassing situations.

Have you come into a little extra cash that you know will burn a hole in your pocket? Instead of spending it, put it in the pocket of your off-season jacket. It will save you from spending it and give you a nice little surprise in a few months when you could need it more.

And of course, keep those recyclables because each item is worth money. You can help your bank account while helping the environment.

6. Explain the envelope system for budgeting. How effective it is?

Here is a neat way to budget your money or learn about the art of budgeting, as long as you are dealing with a relatively small amount. It involves having a significant amount of cash in the house, so plan on purchasing a fireproof safe or a *very* secret drawer somewhere to keep it in. Every time you get paid, split up your cash into envelopes. (Just how many depends on your specific needs and wants.) Try having one for eating out, one for clothing, one for household items, one for auto repairs, one for gifts, one for home improvements, and others for whatever else you might need. This system is not for everyone, especially if you are not able to have money in the house without impulse spending. To see if this method is effective for your lifestyle, start small, using only one or two envelopes, and work up from there.

The disadvantage of this system is that you are not making any interest on your money if it's sitting at home. (Keep in mind that you are not making much interest with it sitting in the savings account either.) To have the best of both worlds, use a "virtual envelope" system. Have your money in the bank but use a spreadsheet listing your total budget and have sub-accounts for each category of expenses. You can easily see where your money is going and track your progress as well.

7. How much money should I have in my emergency fund?

Life has a funny way of playing with people, and usually these games cost money. Ideally the average person should have approximately three to six months of basic living expenses saved up in case anything happens. After all, you don't want a bad situation turning worse because you don't have the cash to compensate.

The more dependants you have, the more you should save. Three months salary may be fine for someone who is single but would not last nearly as long if the person was feeding a family of four. You should also consider the level of difficulty in finding a new job in case you lose yours. For example, if you are a teacher and teachers are in high demand, you probably will not be unemployed for long.

The key to creating and building an emergency fund is putting a little bit aside on a regular basis. This can be arranged with your bank so you don't notice the deduction as much. Whatever your situation looks like, be responsible now and it will save you time, energy, and one heck of a migraine later on.

8. I have automatic withdrawal payments from my bank account. Is it better to have all of my bills paid on the same day or spread the payment dates over the course of the month?

Automatic withdrawal payments can be a very convenient and easy way to pay bills since you don't have to do anything. (isn't it interesting that the one thing banks make easy is *getting rid* of your money?) When you pay these bills is generally up to you and should depend on certain factors. When do you get paid? You could have a number (or all) of your online payments processed on your paydays. You won't have to worry about having an overdrawn account ever again. (Just keep those paychecks higher than your bills!). If you decide to spread your payments out, just be aware of how much money you have consistently over the course of the month.

9. I can't control my impulse buying! It seems like the more I buy, the more I want to buy! HELP!

This is actually a very common problem among people of all income earners. Try to pay cash whenever possible. This way you can literally *see* the money you are spending and you are less likely to empty your wallet or purse. Sometimes, however, that singing clown lamp in the store window is just too tempting to ignore! Well, instead of running inside and throwing money on the counter, write the item down on a card and wait two weeks. If you still want the item (and have the disposable income) then go for it. The trick is not to have any more than three items on the list. If you want to add more, then you have to cross one item off. This will reduce your "got to have it now or I will explode" habits and will also save you from buying things you may regret later. (Clown lamp? What was I THINKING?)

10. My spouse is a habitual over-spender! How can I keep the bills paid and the fridge full?

You will find financial squabbles in every relationship. This is because people approach money and how to budget it differently. Your spouse may simply not understand the importance of budgeting and need guidance. This does NOT mean taking away the credit card and acting superior. In fact, get rid of the negative attitude altogether. It won't help. Try getting your partner to write down his or her life goals, and show your partner how the frivolous spending will never get them to where they want to be. If you have a joint bank account, consider having enough income from his or her paycheck (assuming your partner has one) directly deposited into the joint account for bills and necessities. Your partner must understand that large purchases need to be discussed, and saving money may not be fun, but neither is loads of debt. Frankly, your spouse may not be able to control his or her spending as much as you can, so educate your partner as much as you can on budgeting and financial control. If both parties agree, consider taking over the finances; however, be careful because this can cause conflict down the road. You may consider consulting with a financial planner if you feel a professional would act as a better reference.

Chapter Six

INCREASING EARNING POTENTIAL:
Why Make Some When You Can Make More?

Are you not making enough? Do you ask yourself how you could make more money without sacrificing time and effort? Of course you have; we all have. We've all had that dream of the money tree growing in the backyard that would solve all of our financial woes. This tree may not exist (If you find one, let me know.), but there are practical, effective ways to increase what you make without making huge life adjustments.

1. How can I increase my earning potential while already working full time?

Do you have too many bills and not enough hours in the day? There are several smart ways to fix this without losing sleep. If you are too busy to tackle a part-time job, try starting a small home-based business that doesn't require much time. You can turn a hobby into a profit and have fun working on your own terms. This takes commitment, some time, energy, and a little know-how, so if that isn't for you, try upgrading your education. Taking night or weekend courses is a great way to increase your earning potential because you can build your resume and learn different ways to become successful as well as open doors you never knew existed. Education is always a good investment and can be enjoyable too.

2. Is pawning my possessions a good way to make some quick cash?

Having an out-of-money experience? Though pawning your things is definitely a quick way of making some money, it is probably not the best way. If you want to sell your possessions, chances are your friends or family would buy them from you for more money than a pawnshop would offer. If you intend to buy back your possessions, remember your money has to come from somewhere, and pawnshops usually charge a high interest rate. If you decide to sell your things to a pawnshop, keep in mind there is no such thing as a good deal!

3. How important is personal image in creating business opportunity?

Recent studies show that our behavior and the way we conduct business can be attributed in part to unknown processes. That is why the first impression we make is always important. Eye contact is integral when making business deals. It shows you are personable, trustworthy, and confident in your ability. A person is more likely to trust and invest money in somebody if they like him or her as a person. After eye contact, smell plays an active role in your business appeal. If your body is sending out the wrong signals (such as body odor, cigarette smoke, or even foot smell), people can build up a negative picture of you without even knowing why. You do not want to take this chance when networking and creating business opportunity. So keep up the hygiene! Your image includes your speech, so be aware of your audience at all times. It's nice to be funny, but everyone has a different sense of humour, so be careful. You do not want to say or do something that puts off people conducting business with you. Usually they won't tell you exactly why and you're left making the same mistakes time and time again.

4. What affect does my health have on my financial status?

This is a very complicated question because along with many x-factors, there is no one right answer or multiple right answers for that matter. Speaking generally, physical fitness does affect your financial fitness in a number of ways. First of all, unhealthy addictions such as drinking and smoking can make you less of a performer at work. For instance, you usually do not work as well hung-over as when you had a good night's rest. Financially, the costs add up. If you were to buy a pack of cigarettes every day at $10 (CDN), it would cost you $3,650 a year. An average of a few drinks at $5 (CDN) a day would cost you $5,475. That's just under $10,000 a year!

Typically, smell (including cigarette smell) can affect business relationships with new clients. Depending on the business, actual physical fitness can help a person's confidence, which is an advantage in business relations. Your diet as well can have a great deal to do with your focus and attitude in the workplace. Candy and fast food will make you crash and burn, but supplying fruits and vegetables to eat throughout the day will actually keep you focused and energized. (An apple will actually wake you up more effectively than a cup of coffee!) Though it is certainly not necessary for a person to be physically fit to be financially fit, a person may exude confidence and energy that can increase networking skills and lead to prosperous opportunities.

5. What advice can I give my children to make sure they become financially independent?

Teaching your children about smart financing is best taught through example. Young people learn best through observation, experience, and habit, which if you are consistent with your own saving methods will be ingrained in them simply by watching.

For younger children, most money they receive will be small coins, so why not set up a piggy bank? If they want to save up for something, a bicycle for example, you can place a picture of one on the piggy bank and they will be more likely to stay motivated to save. Also, have them count their savings every month or so to demonstrate their accumulation. A great incentive is to match any amount your child saves. For every ten dollars, you match with ten dollars. If this works, try adding interest payments to their savings, offering fifty cents for every ten dollars they save. Your child will learn the basics of interest, as well as stay motivated to save money. You can set up an award system (It does not have to be a money system.) where each chore completed by the child means a star, sticker, or bauble, etc. This way the child will feel accomplished by receiving awards for good behaviour and hard work.

Once your children get older, they may need some more advanced guidance, so why not set up a savings chart on the fridge tracking how much they need to save in order to achieve their financial goals. This will act as a visual reminder and can explain step by step how to become financially independent. You can also set up a savings account, using the opportunity to explain the process to them. You can also encourage them to perform chores around the house for their allowance, such as mowing the lawn, shovelling snow, etc. By incorporating incentives for earning money, children will learn the value of what they earn and will more likely go on to work hard in the real world toward achieving these same ends. Material incentives aren't necessary; knowing they can become successful by working hard is the key, so do anything you can to increase their self-esteem and work ethic!

6. What are some different kinds of unclaimed property?

Has a friend ever repaid you that twenty dollars you forgot you had lent them? Wouldn't it be nice to experience that surprise on a potentially much larger scale? The truth is there may be hundreds if not thousands of dollars worth of property or money that you are entitled to. Most unclaimed property becomes abandoned because of a change of address, change of name (due to marriage), or death of the owner. There are many situations that can result in lost or abandoned money—anything from having checks mailed to the wrong address to simply forgetting that you are owed money. Unclaimed property can include the following:

-Dormant Savings and Checking Accounts and Certificates of Deposit

-Safe Deposit Box Contents

-Un-cashed Money Orders, Cashiers Checks, and Travellers Checks

-Un-cashed Payroll Checks

-Unused Gift Certificates

-Oil and Gas Royalty Payments

-Un-cashed Stock and Mutual Fund Dividends

-Stock Certificates

-Mineral Royalty Payments

-Unclaimed Security Deposits

-Utility Deposits

-Customer Deposits, Overpayments, Credit Balances, and Refunds

-Court Deposits

-Insurance Payments

-Probate Court Judgments

-Overlooked Property

-Paid-Up Life Insurance Policies

-Un-cashed Death Benefit Checks and Life Insurance Proceeds

-Health and Accident Insurance Payments

7. How can I find out if there is unclaimed money or property owed to me?

Even if you are certain nothing is owed to you, it may be worth the short amount of time it takes to check. You can call or write the unclaimed property office in each province or state in which you or any of your deceased relatives have lived. You can sometimes also contact these offices online. The representative will ask you for your name, social insurance/security number, address, and any previous addresses where you've lived in that area. They will ask the same information regarding anyone who is a legal beneficiary. If there is a match, you simply have to prove that you are who you say you are, and behold! You have just claimed your money with no charge! In addition, if the search comes up with nothing, try again in a few years. You never know what you could be missing out on.

A warning: do not pay someone a finder's fee for locating your lost property! If the process is this simple, why would you give up a percentage of your entitlement, or worse, a flat fee up front? It may be more convenient, but the commission can be outrageous.

8. Are there government grants for the average person? How can I get one?

Grants are not provided simply to fatten your wallet or pay off debt. There are obligations that accompany each grant, but yes, they are available to almost anyone. There are obvious obstacles, however. The number of government grants is small and competition is massive, so take the pursuit of the money seriously with a business plan and future goals. First you must apply for a grant through a grant office, including your objectives, and then a review will be made through a committee, with a comparison of your proposal to similar ones that also need to be reviewed. Accessing a grant is also contingent on a number of factors. It would be a smart idea to find out the specifics in where you live. Grants are generally given out to non-profit organizations, local governments, and target groups with specific requirements such as transportation. Assistance is also given to sports athletes.

9. How can I make money off of my vehicle?

I doubt there are many ways you can literally *make* money off of your vehicle, as this is an asset that is sure to depreciate in value the second you drive it off the lot. However, there are some opportunities that a vehicle makes accessible that you can take on. For example, you could always deliver pizza or newspapers. The most prosperous way you could make money off your vehicle is to provide a service for elderly people or people otherwise unable to drive, providing trips to the grocery store, pharmacy, school, and other places. You would make some money, provide a much-needed service, and maybe even make a friend or two.

10. What are some ways to make money online?

For those who know how to harness it, the power and opportunity the Internet has to offer is massive and still has room to grow. The Web offers a plethora of opportunities to make money, but the trick is to recognize the legitimate ways versus the scams. Just like any other moneymaking venture, you have to be smart and aware of what you are doing.

First you can sell things on the Net. Sites offer online auctions, which are a great way to spring clean and can turn into a lucrative hobby. Teaching online can be very profitable as well, but most likely you would need to partner up with a local school or university. Finally, filling out surveys can bring in a few bucks (maximum one entry per survey).

If you own a company or small business, the possibilities of making money online become even greater. If you don't have a Web site of your own or want to expand your demographic, there are sites that you can become a part of that actually help sell your product. If you do own a Web site, you can sell other people's products that you think your audience may be interested in. You will receive a certain commission after the sale or subscription is completed. Advertising is also an excellent way to broadcast your services over the net and make money. You can join an advertising network, which sell banner ads and offer advertising space.

11. I have a great idea for a new invention that will make me rich! What do I do now?

Looking to revolutionize the world with your new invention? Having an idea for a product that will make you money is great, but it won't get you rich. The truth is, if you ask, most people have at least one or two ideas of their own. The trick is to first find out if people would buy it and then get up off the couch and do something about it. First you need a patent. A patent is a legal document that ensures the inventor (you) the exclusive right to commercially develop and distribute the product for the life of the patent (typically twenty years), excluding others from making or distributing it. To get a patent, you need to make sure there isn't already an invention like yours out there. Certain Web sites offer search archives with this information, or you can contact the patent office near you. Patenting a product can be a lengthy and confusing process, so be ready for it.

The patent is just the first step. Next comes research and development, engineering, commercialization, and distribution. And you need money for all of it. Grants may cover much of the costs, but they may not. Generally speaking, creating and developing an invention is not for the faint of heart, but if you are *committed* to doing it, then do as much research on the industry as possible and go for it. Who knows. Maybe that musical motorized deodorant applicator will make you millions. (There *are* crazier things.)

12. What are some types of charitable donations that qualify for tax exemptions?

There are many tax credits that apply when donating to a charity, though the charity must *qualify* for taxation purposes, which is easy enough to find out on the Internet or through the association itself. The donations are added to other personal credits under the Income Tax Act and are deducted directly from taxes owed. You can deduct donations of cash, real estate, vehicles, residual interest, insurance policies, mileage, and lottery funding. Cash donations result in non-refundable tax credits. The credit equals around 15.25 percent marginal tax rate on the first two hundred dollars of your donations, and anything in excess of two hundred dollars will be calculated at the highest marginal tax rate (around 29 percent). Tax benefits work as incentives for donations, so if you have an old car or are just feeling generous, keep charitable associations in mind!

13. I won the lottery! Woo hoo! But it's divided, so I only get a little bit each year. Is there anything I can do to get all the money at once?

It's your lucky day. Not only did you win the lottery, you *can* get it in one large lump sum. The way normal settlements work—and this applies to lotteries, lawsuit claims, any large *contractual* amount—is you receive your funding in stages. Say you won $25 million; it could work out that you would receive $1 million a year for twenty-five years. If that works for you, then great! Enjoy! If you don't want to wait the twenty-five years or if you find that $20 million dog collar too hard to resist, then there is a way to speed up the entire process and claim your money now. Private lending institutions like some credit companies provide a service of structured settlements. You sign with them and the institution will give you all the money right on the spot! However, these places usually take a little off the top for commission, so you might end up with $24 million instead. So basically it's up to you. Do you want $25 million at the end of your life or $24 million now?

14. I am a full-time university student. How can I make or save money?

Being a university student can take up a lot of your time. However, if you can get a part-time job without having it interfere with your schoolwork, give it a shot. There are many job opportunities right on campus that are convenient. Otherwise, if you want to make money, you've got to get creative. Assuming you are not worried about student loans and you simply want to make money to save or spend (I would suggest saving.), concentrate on ways to save on books. Campus prices are ridiculously expensive, so share with a classmate or try finding the same books at stores off campus or even online to save costs. Also sell your textbooks back to the school at the end of each course. Chances are you will never reference them again (unless it is applicable to other courses), and you can clear up some space in your dorm room or home. Usually this is a consignment process, meaning you'll get the money once your books are sold. Depending on what major you hold, you can try borrowing class books from the campus library instead of buying them. This can save you hundreds of dollars over a few years. University is a time to feel independent, so make sure you focus on a financial plan to help you do just that. Chances are if you start saving now, you will have a better chance at saving when you're older.

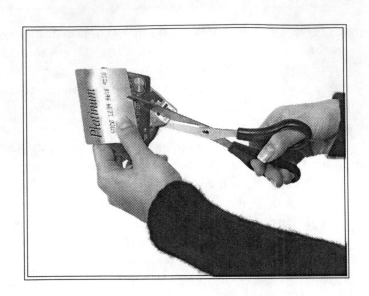

Chapter Seven

CUTTING COSTS:
Easy Saving Tips That You Can Use on a Daily Basis

YOU SHOULD MAKE MORE MONEY THAN YOU SPEND. Sure it's a simple enough statement to say, but it's not so simple to live by. Many people get caught up in the spending game and forget about the consequences of living beyond their means. A good way to live within your budget and still have many of the things you love is by cutting the fat off of necessary (and not so necessary) costs. Sometimes spending more, especially when you can't afford it, is just plain dumb.

The one thing every person should know about his or her financial life is that saving money does not have to be hard. Inconvenient? Time-consuming? Even boring? Sure. Difficult?

No way. In fact, there are ways to save money every day that take no effort at all. Basically we're talking short-term adjustments for long-term objectives.

Begin by reviewing where your finances are going and if the things you are spending money on are really worth it. If they aren't, trim the fat and chances are your life won't be much different, just richer. Many people struggle with saving money in the short term since they don't see the savings right away. They assume it's not happening, which simply isn't true. A few cents off milk may not be much, but think about how much milk you drink a year!

1. How can I cut costs on food?

Food is a necessary expense; don't feel guilty or worried about spending money on the things that will keep you alive! The trick is being smart about where you're spending it and how you can avoid spending more money than you have to. Consider the grocery store. Clipping coupons is always a penny-saving venture and is usually worth the effort in the long run. Some stores have double or triple coupon days, which could make the difference. Also, make a shopping list that you can stick to prior to visiting the grocery store (no more impulse buying), and never go food shopping when you're hungry! Your financial priorities tend to waiver when temptation is all around you. Do not eat out or order in food often. The convenience will cost you big money in the long run. Fruits, vegetables, and basic food ingredients are usually inexpensive, so buy in bulk and make your own meals at home; make extra so there's leftovers for lunch and some you can freeze. By using vegetables that you've grown and doing the cooking yourself, you are saving money, and who knows; maybe you'll discover the chef within! Lastly, compare store prices. This is an excellent way to save on food costs and is not all that difficult. You can look through flyers (Some stores even post their flyers on their Web sites.) or try different stores and compare in person. Though this does seem time-intensive, the research and effort you put in will definitely save you money and make you feel like a money-saving superhero!

To cut down on the cost of drinks, avoid the expensive name brands. Also cut down on alcohol. You will save a bundle of money and feel great, too. Drink water when you can. (You're paying for it anyway.) Try keeping a jug of water in your fridge so there is always a cheap alternative when you're thirsty.

2. How can I save money when eating out?

When eating in a restaurant, there are tips you can use to keep from spending a fortune while still enjoying a night out. Check local newspapers for coupons or deals for restaurants you've been dying to try. If the restaurant is expensive, try visiting for lunch or dessert. The prices are usually smaller, and you still get the experience of a fancy restaurant. Also try asking if there are half-portions available on menu items, and don't be afraid to take some food home for lunch the next day. Be aware of what you're drinking. Alcohol can be very expensive, so if you don't care what you're drinking, go with water with lemon or lime. Try not to eat out often, as this will certainly create a dent in your budget!

3. How can I avoid spending lots of money on clothing?

Nobody says you have to shop at premium, top-dollar stores for your clothing. If you are looking to save a buck or two, there are many second-hand stores you can try that offer cheap and eclectic fashions for all shapes and sizes. The assortments change often too, so if you can't find anything you like, try again in a week. If you are strapped for cash, there are charitable services that can help you, like the Salvation Army, Goodwill, or your local church.

If you are looking to simply resist your shopaholic tendencies, try skipping the brand new "must-have" accessories. What is popular today is old news tomorrow, so save the credit card debt. If you can sew or know somebody who can, then go nuts! Get creative and make repairing or altering your clothes a fun new hobby! It will also cut down on replacement costs. Turning your clothes inside out before you wash them tends to keep the color from fading.

4. What about shelter? How can I cut costs?

Shelter is a little more difficult to cut costs. You can always expect the unexpected to occur. If the furnace breaks or the pipes burst, you cannot ignore it or cover it up with duct tape. However, there are a few simple ways to reduce costs. Begin by setting up a house emergency fund for any problems that come up that you cannot fix yourself. When something does need repairing, do your research and compare contractors. They are in direct competition with each other and their rates are relatively fluid, so get the best price. This does not mean the *lowest* price, however. Generally you get what you paid for and you want the work done properly. If you are looking to remodel, take your time and do each room on its own. You will save on costs and save yourself a headache—or two or three.

5. Is there any way to save money on air conditioning?

Believe it or not, there are plenty of easy ways to reduce costs on cooling your home. Begin by investing in the right air conditioner, and make sure that it is serviced properly to ensure efficient use. Look for one that has a SEER number (seasonal energy efficiency ratio) of thirteen or better. Remember, if you own a window air-conditioning unit, that a large size doesn't equal cost efficiency! Instead, base the size of the machine on the size of the room, and remember not to block it with furniture. A programmable thermostat will pay for itself by not performing at full capacity while you're away from the house for a while. For less costly ways to save, you can install awnings on the sunny side of your house, or close the curtains. Planting trees and shrubs around your house can reduce the heat from the sun while cutting costs up to 30 percent. Also try closing the cooling ducts and doors to rooms you aren't using. Be aware of items in your home that generate heat. This includes office equipment, lighting, cooking equipment, dishwashers, and clothes washers. Remember a little awareness and some common sense go a long way when the energy bill arrives.

6. What are some ways to save money on heating costs?

Heating your home is usually necessary, and if you live in a cold climate you know how expensive it can be. Luckily there are some simple ways to cut costs without spending a dime. Firstly, you don't have to heat every room in your house, so shut the doors and vents to rooms you barely use. In the rooms you do spend time in, turn down the heat and use space heaters instead. Washing clothes in cold water helps, and by cutting your shower time a little, you can actually save up to 33 percent on your hot water costs! Keep your curtains open so the sun can shine in and heat your home naturally. And remember, if you are ever a little chilly, putting on a warm sweater is much cheaper than turning up the thermostat. (You can even put it in the clothes dryer for a few minutes to really get cozy!) By following these tips, you'll be sure to get those warm, fuzzy feelings when your heating bill arrive.

7. How can I save on energy costs?

There are lots of easy ways to reduce energy in your home that will save you money and have you feeling clever for doing so. Turn off your clothes dryer about ten minutes before the end of the cycle. You'll save money and your clothes will continue to dry in the warm machine. If something minor does break around the house, try fixing it yourself. Just because you've never done it before doesn't mean you can't! With some research and a little confidence, you may end up saving lots of money on professionals. (Otherwise, keep close the number of a friend who does handiwork. Friends are always cheaper than hired help.) Your computer screen uses up more than half the energy of the computer, and a 17 inch computer screen uses 35 percent more energy than a 14 inch screen, so use the smallest screen that fits your need, and turn it off when it's not in use. Another thing to keep in mind is that a chest freezer is more energy efficient than a stand-up one because the stand-up one lets less cold air escape when you open the door.

8. How can I save money on my phone bill?

In this age of portable *everything*, it is easier than ever to keep chatting everywhere you go, but a plan that works for your neighbour may not work for you. Keep in mind landlines (phone lines connected to your house) may operate a little differently than cell phones because they usually involve different service providers. Begin by sitting down with your phone statements from the last two to three months and figure out your talking pattern. How much is long-distance? What time of day do you talk the most? Once you have a good idea of your phone habits, contact your telephone company and have them help you pick a plan that works best. There are plans that provide cheaper rates in the evenings and weekends or on long-distance calls. Buy a phone card to keep on hand when you need it. Because of the competition in service providers, there are always new plan offers out there, so shop around and you can end up saving lots of money. If you are a fan of sending text messages on your cell phone but hate the high prices, you can send free texts via the Internet. Just go to the phone provider's website and type it out. Your friend will receive the message on his or her phone at no cost to you! Always think of your service provider as working for *you*, and you'll have a much easier time when that bill comes your way.

9. Gas is getting more expensive by the day! Is there any way to predict when prices will go up?

Wouldn't it be great if you had a warning at the pump telling you when to fill up before gas prices skyrocket? Well, in case your crystal ball is broken, here are some tips to help you save some cash. Though it is extremely difficult to predict and fluctuates day to day, the price of gas is a commodity just like everything else and is subject to similar factors. Rising prices, inflation, and tax laws (past and present) can all be studied to generally predict how the gas trend will continue. Not a math whiz? You don't need graphs and laser pointers to figure out that it's all about supply and demand. Demand is steadily rising due to the increase in population and number of cars per household. A smart way to save money on gas is to check the Internet. Many cities have sites that track local gas prices so you can compare and track where the cheapest price is that day. Stock up! If you find a great price for gas, fill up a proper container before the price jumps back up. (Keep in mind it could always go lower, too.) The thing to remember is that the higher the demand and competition, the higher the price of gas. This is why large cities generally set gas at a slightly higher rate than smaller towns.

10. What are some more ways I can cut down on fuel costs?

There are many ways to save money on gas and avoid lining up at the gas station more often than you have to. In fact, just by making sure your vehicle is properly maintained, you can cut up to 10 percent of your fuel cost. Low tires, dirty oil, clogged air filters, and poorly tuned engines all increase your gas consumption. Secondly, by using a block heater on cold winter days, you can save as much as 10 to 20 percent on fuel costs! Also when you are on the road, have a plan to go everywhere you need to in one trip, while remembering not to idle. Further, never underestimate the benefits of carpooling! You could potentially save $400 - $700 a year. Lastly, you can always purchase vehicles that aren't gas-powered, or run on a low amount of gas. A hybrid car specializes in saving fuel consumption, and for short trips to the grocery store, a scooter or bicycle may be a good investment for you while saving on fuel.

11. Are there ways to buy cheap air travel tickets?

If you're looking to buy airfare but are turned off by the prices, don't worry just yet. There are ways to lower the cost of your airfare and make the best out of a usually expensive situation. First, booking your flight in advance and being flexible with your dates will help you take advantage of seat sales. If you travel on slow days— Tuesdays and Wednesday's usually—or stay over on a Saturday, this will also help lower costs. If you are looking to go on vacation, it will save you a bundle if you travel to your destination in the off-season. (It would help you avoid crowds, too.) If you can, travel on late flights in coach (a little less leg room, a lot less money). Avoiding direct travel will save you cash too. When booking your flight, tell the reservation clerk you are willing to be bumped to the next available flight. For getting on the following flight, you will receive a cash discount voucher for a future flight. Also offer to go standby on sold-out flights. Chances are you will get a seat anyway and you'll pay a lot less for it.

These suggestions may sound a little inconvenient, but in the long run these tips could end up saving you hundreds of dollars in just one trip. Imagine how much you would save on *every* trip you take! You could fly yourself somewhere nice with the money you save!

12. What are some smart ways to save money on shopping retail?

The trick to saving money while still getting the things you want lies in a little advanced planning. High demand equals high prices, so consider the time of year in relation to *all* of your purchases. Spring and summer merchandise usually goes on sale in June or July and fall and winter items usually are put on the clearance shelves around January, so be smart and do your shopping then. Besides, in the winter you probably already know whether you need a lawnmower, so don't procrastinate or it'll cost you!

Try shopping online to cut down on costs. There are plenty of sites that offer overstocked merchandise or retail and grocery stores that offer their services online. Not only would you save on time and gasoline, sometimes you can even enter in promotion or coupon codes and save money while still in your living room! There are even Web sites that specifically focus on coupons for all kinds of merchandise. Now that's smart buying!

13. Is it better to lease or own a car?

This depends on how and how long you intend on using the car. When you lease you are not paying for the car itself, only its projected depreciation while it is in your use. Typically this ranges from twenty-four to forty-eight months. Many people who lease eventually pay more because they focus only on the monthly payments and not on the car's worth. Leasing usually comes with mileage restrictions, not to mention security deposits. Once you turn in your leased vehicle, there are several fees including "wear and tear" and a payment making up any distance you exceeded from the mileage agreement.

So many times leasing isn't the cheapest way to go. If you can't afford to buy the car you're after, you can purchase it with a long-term loan, which is generally less costly than leasing. You can also consider buying an older used car.

As with any large purchase, understanding the deal before you sign anything is essential to driving away in confidence. Study the agreement and if you have any questions, ask! Jargon and technical aspects of the agreement may be confusing, so do not let the salesperson talk around or above you. This is your deal, your vehicle, and your money!

14. Is hiring an accountant to do my taxes worth the money, or am I better off grinding through it myself?

It depends on how experienced you are in regard to your country's tax system and how complicated your taxes get. Generally speaking, I would hire a professional to do your taxes, as it's their business and you want your taxes done right, especially if you have a complicated tax return. If you have a basic return, you can buy a program and do it yourself for much less, but you may have to wait for your refund check to come in the mail and this could take a long time. If you need the money right away, go use a tax professional who can get you a check at the same time as filing your tax return.

15. I am expecting a baby. How will this affect my finances?

As the saying goes, parents are those who carry around pictures of their kids in their wallets, right where their money used to be. It's true that a bundle of joy can also bring with it a bundle of expenses, so the more you can do to prepare and be aware of these expenses, the better off you are. A new baby can "cost" as much as $32,000 for the first two years alone, so it's a good idea to know what you're getting into before you become a parent. These expenses include everything from cribs to day care, to food, to diapers. Obviously having a new small relative in the house is not cheap! Definitely try to save up for this life change, or consider a new budget for living once the new little one arrives. And don't expect them to get any cheaper. Depending on your lifestyle, a child could cost up to $9,000 and $10,000 a year until the age of 17!

16. A baby is expensive! What can I do to reduce these costs while still providing a good upbringing?

Being a parent is enough hard work without having to worry about financial strains as well. This is where forward-looking arrangements come into play. In the United States, maternity leave benefits last up to six months; in Canada it can be up to one year. Consult your workplace regarding any company-provided benefit plans that have to do with infant care and pediatric coverage. This can significantly reduce out-of-pocket expenses and lessen the worry when and if your child needs medical attention.

If you are expecting a child, that automatically gives you at least nine months to make a realistic and reasonable financial plan. A smart way to reduce costs when expecting or raising a small child is obvious. Hand-me-downs and thrift-store items are a great way to cut costs and can offer discounts on anything from cribs to clothing, to toys. Besides, your baby will not know or care if his or her crib has had a previous owner; neither should you. You can make your own baby food (which is also healthier) and make your own baby furniture. (Nothing says *I love you* like a homemade mobile!) If you need day care, find out if there is a less costly (but certified) childcare provider in your community. This will be cheaper and more convenient for you on a day-to-day basis.

Truth be told, any expense you spend on your baby can be easily justified and will always be worth the price you pay for having a baby. (The same can be said for childbirth, but let's not go there!) What is most important to decide is what the baby needs versus what you want the baby to have. Spoiling your child when you do not have the means to do so doesn't help anything and is actually a common cause for debt problems, so don't let it happen to you.

Chapter Eight

IDENTITY THEFT:
Signposts to Watch for on the Information Highway

In this fast-paced world of technology, e-commerce is definitely here to stay and has become a simple, quick, and convenient way to check your accounts, transfer funds, pay bills, and track transactions. The luxury of having your personal information available to you at a moment's notice certainly beats standing in line at the bank. However, with every good invention come those who want to exploit it. As a responsible online user, you must be aware and proceed cautiously to effectively protect your personal business.

Being a victim of identity theft can be a costly problem, both in time and expense. Victims spend time fixing their credit reports and closing bad accounts while establishing new ones, and it becomes more difficult to obtain a loan and even a job.

1. What are the dangers of online banking?

Online banking can be a fairly safe practice as long as you are careful of what you are doing and keep updated on scams and dangers. Banking sites utilize encryption software, which makes your information inaccessible until it is "unlocked," or decrypted.

Always be cautious of how much information you give online. Personal information that you assume to be safe through certain corporations *can be sold* to data brokers who will use it for database filing. Make sure the site you are using has guarantees against this. Be aware! Banking sites never send out unsolicited emails requesting personal information! E-mails like these mimic real, professional sites and, unless you are careful, can access important information about you or manipulate settings such as IP addresses and computer settings. Do not open these e-mails!

2. How can I reduce the risk of online identity theft?

E-mail, unlike banking sites, is not usually encrypted, so never send mail with account numbers, credit card numbers, or any other personal information. As well, always sign out of online accounts. Logging out once you are leaving a Web site is like locking the door (your password being the key). In addition, when discarding computers, do it safely. Destroy any disc, CD, or DVD that may have personal information on it. When replacing your computer system, delete all information on your hard drive. Keep in mind that deleting a file is not enough! It can still be accessed, so be sure to use a "white-space wiper" program to wipe out access to these "deleted" files. Finally, remember to carefully review your credit card statement each month for any unauthorized purchases or charges made on your behalf. If you notice some suspicious activity, contact your bank or credit card company immediately.

If you still feel uncomfortable using your credit card online or performing any financial transactions, here are some ways to protect yourself. Always make sure your browser is the latest, most updated version. This takes advantage of any encryption capabilities. In addition to this, install a firewall and have updated spyware software installed in your computer. Look for a padlock symbol in the upper or lower corner of the Web page; this icon indicates that the page is secure. Also, look for an S after the usual http url. This also indicates a secure server.

3. How can I reduce the risk of becoming a victim of other kinds of identity theft?

Though you cannot eliminate the risk completely, there are steps you can take to reduce the risk of identity theft. Always keep updated identification documents in a safe place. This includes photocopies of all cards inside your wallet or purse. This will not protect you from fraud but will save you a headache if anything happens to the information. As well, know whom you are giving information to. This means verifying the identity of the person requesting your information, especially if *they* contacted *you*. Remember to destroy personal information when you no longer need it. Identity thieves are garbage-pickers! This includes all account statements, old identification cards, and loan applications. A paper shredder may be a wise investment for your home. Evaluate your wallet or purse and keep any unnecessary information at home. Not only will losing this information increase your chances of identity theft, it will cost you time and money to replace these documents. If anything is lost or stolen, report it immediately! Reporting the loss of debit or credit cards reduces the risk of others using it and racking up your account balance. For extra insurance, limit personal information on a check. Have your initials printed on the cheque and never write down the complete account number. And finally, always protect your passwords! Shield keypads when entering any password in public and choose a password that is difficult to guess, changing these passwords often.

Chapter Nine

Finances and the Workplace:
How to Keep Your Income Incoming

A large part of maximizing your income potential comes from your attitude. There will be times when you will be fully justified in quitting on the spot or will feel the money you make just doesn't equal the amount of suffering you put up with. These are the times when you should be most aware of factors you may not at first consider. In fact, your emotions have more to do with your workplace stability than your job skills. How do people perceive you? How do you perceive others? How much room do you have to be creative or flexible in your work? These all contribute to your job satisfaction and will affect your long-term standing in your workplace.

Employees should love what they do. But sometimes this doesn't mean they love what they're getting paid. In times like these, you should keep in mind that there is more to income than simple salary. In fact, there are ways to increase your earning potential in the workplace without all that nasty hard work and overtime. It doesn't matter what industry you work in. You can begin making the money you want by being aware of your opportunities to assure financial stability long after you have to worry about working at all.

1. What do successful businesses look for when reviewing an applicant?

Every business seeks out different things when considering an applicant for a position. The person must be a good fit for the company, so research the corporation and the job before you enter an interview. Know what they are looking for. This shows you are interested in the position and consider your work seriously. Depending on the industry, you may need to concentrate on purely professional experience, whereas attitude and personality play a major role if you are applying for a job in the service industry. Generally, however, there are some quick dos and don'ts that always apply. DO be on time. DO be polite. DO dress nicely and cleanly. This applies to your general hygiene as well. DO NOT have your first question be, How much does it pay? This shows your priorities are to yourself, not to the company.

As for the resume, different employers look for different things but experience is always an asset. Remember to include dates, names, and places. Obviously educational background is a must for most businesses, and you should also include any scholarships or awards you've received. Include as well any interests or hobbies you may have. It shows the employer that you are well rounded and fun. Generally, include any relevant information to the business on your resume and include a cover letter introducing yourself to the employer (Research their name!) and why you are interested in the job. Include as well a reference sheet, or make one available upon request. These should not be names of family or friends, but include past employers or anybody who can vouch for past working experience. To really make yourself stand out above the other interviewees, send a letter to the interviewer thanking them for their time a day or two after the meeting.

2. In a job interview, how do you answer that inevitable question, What are your *weaknesses?*

Almost every interview you will go to will include some version of this question. Strengths are easy, but when answering a question about your "weaknesses," the trick is to be honest without trapping yourself in a corner. Say something that is true and specific but wouldn't really apply to the job you are applying for. A great answer is "I work myself too hard," "I take my job too seriously sometimes," or my personal favorite, "I am a perfectionist!" Never say anything like "I can't work with other people" or "I am never on time." That's like saying "Goodbye. I'm completely incompetent." A good idea is to note that you are constantly working on your weaknesses and use them as a way to improve yourself. The interviewer will respect you for being honest, and you don't end up looking like a weak employee.

3. I'm going to ask my boss for a raise. How should I prepare?

Asking your employer for a pay increase can be a very nerve-racking and stressful chore, but every once in awhile you need to take off the gloves and get dirty. You are essentially selling yourself and your abilities to someone who may not necessarily want to shell out extra company cash, so be diligent, confident, and above all, professional.

Always do your research prior to confrontation. Find out what other people at the company who are in your field are making. It may be rude to ask your peers, so try online for current salary information. Next evaluate how financially sound your employer is. The easiest thing a boss can say to turn you down is that they just don't have the cash. Knowing the financial health of the business can tell you when a good time to ask would be, and any financial research you gather could help you in arguing your case. Next step: prepare your argument and decide what you're worth. Consider the amount of years you have spent with the company and any extra responsibilities you have taken on without compensation. List these duties as well as the relevant skills that make you successful at your job. The next thing you should consider is what you are willing to do if you're turned down or are given a smaller raise than expected. Are you going to quit your job? (This information is for you. Don't give your boss an ultimatum. This is negative confrontation and does not make you look smart or professional.) If there are specific reasons as to why you were turned down, consider any changes you can make to elevate your job performance and ask to review the situation in time. Finally, make an appointment with your boss. (You never want to bombard him or her in the hallway or cafeteria.) Remember to be aggressive yet positive, and confident yet focused. Good luck!

4. I'm too scared to ask for a raise! What are some things I can do around the office to motivate my boss into noticing me?

I'm assuming this question does not include the working-hard solution? Truth be told, there are some tricks that can put you on the top of the boss's list, without working your fingers to the bone or even being the staff suck-up. If you work in an office environment, always be on time and keep an active, up-to-date schedule of what you're working on. That way if you are ever interrogated about a project you worked on three weeks ago, you can spill out details as if the project meant a lot to you! As well, many offices will re-evaluate compensation at your annual performance review. If they don't, then mention it. Chances are they won't fire you for asking.

Get to know your boss, even if it means spending time out of the workplace. This will depend on the boss you have, but it will not only give you an advantage in knowing what your boss is looking for specifically, but it will let him or her know that you take a personal interest in his or her life. Remember not to get too personal, however. You don't want to overstep any boundaries!

And if you run your own business, then you are your own boss, so stop reading and give yourself a raise already!

5. What should I be aware of when setting up a retirement plan?

You should begin by assessing your life situation. Find out if your place of work has a pension or retirement plan in place and whether or not you are eligible. Next find out how much these plans would be worth when you do retire. This will tell you how much you need to save, if at all, in addition to these benefits. Does your employer offer a matching contribution to your retirement plan? If so, contribute what you can because it will one day offer a 100 percent return! Also, find out what happens to your company retirement plan if you change jobs. Sometimes these benefits can be transferred into an IRA or cashed in. Lastly, discuss whether or not your health and life insurance policies are active once you retire, and consider whether or not your Social Security or Social Insurance could reduce your retirement benefits. Discuss this with your employer. Finally, your retirement plan should be reviewed periodically to ensure it is working the way you need it to. The closer you get to retirement age, the more aware you should be of how your plan is performing. The sooner you work these issues out, the less you'll have to worry about when you do retire, so don't procrastinate!

6. I'm ready to retire. What now?

Finally going to retire? Congratulations! Now consider a few things to help ease you into the life of active luxury. Start by reviewing your original retirement goals. Do they still apply? Any illnesses or investment plans can alter your initial expectations. Look at your income. Is it more or less than what you originally set up in your plan? Also consider any outside or additional income to invest. What about spending habits? You may have changed the way you spend money since you set up the plan, so either alter your spending or alter your plan. Next review your investment portfolio. As you are getting ready to retire, it is a good idea to know just how well those investments are performing. Now request a statement of earnings from the Social Security Administration or Social Insurance Administration. This will tell you how much you can expect to earn during retirement and reveal any mistakes that may be in your account.

7. What are some tips to consider if I lose my job?

Being prepared for financial crisis does not mean being paranoid. It's a smart idea to work out a forward-looking plan regarding what could happen if you suddenly lost your job. If you haven't figured out your financial situation, do so, and make sure to include an emergency fund that would get you through at least three months worth of basic expenses. Then compare it against your job stability. Is your job secure? How in demand is it? How easy would it be to find a new job? Next inquire about your job's severance policies and other benefits that you are entitled to if you are laid off.

If you do lose your job, do not burn your bridges, as much as you might like doing so! Apply for unemployment insurance as soon as possible. Also resist the temptation to charge every little thing on your credit card! Finally, keep your job search organized and efficient. It may take time to find new financial sources, so be aggressive in your search and stay motivated.

Chapter Ten

The Bank and You:
Understanding Your Savings

The relationship you have with your bank can say a lot about your finances. Do you trust the bank to make financial choices? How much control do you really have over your money? What are your interest rates and how can you make them better? Your bank must always work toward your best interests. Sometimes simply knowing which questions to ask can save you lots of money.

1. What are the advantages and disadvantages of having a bank savings account?

A savings account is a safe place to put your money. It is easily accessible when you need it and there are no fees or minimum balances. It can also link directly to your checking account, enabling you to transfer funds between the two or have bills paid directly from the account. The only real disadvantage of a savings account is the low interest rate (low risk = low return).

2. How long do I keep old bank statements?

If you are self-employed, you should keep all bank statements accounting for the last seven years. Otherwise, keep them for two years. Have a safe place for them and keep them organized in case you need to reference them later on.

3. Why do governments audit people? Is it a completely random process?

Government auditing is a very detailed examination of financial records to check the accuracy of those records. The process verifies a person's transactions and financial statements, making sure there are no outstanding discrepancies. A certain number of people or organizations are more likely to get audited, including lending institutions that contribute to or are active in federally sponsored loan programs such as education and housing. In every audit, the auditor must abide by the government auditing standards, which generally include responsible overview of Internet control, consistency review, recommendations for corrective action, and proper reporting procedures. Random audits do happen, but you are more likely to be audited if you have returns that vary from year to year or all of a sudden receive a large refund, for example. Software and staff are developed to spot these red flag situations.

4. Should married couples have separate bank accounts or a joint account?

Approximately 50 percent of marriages end in divorce, and most of the cases cite financial problems as the root cause. Considering this, the issue of money—who has it, where it goes, who has access, and so on—should be discussed and discussed and discussed before the vows are made and the cake is cut. It comes down to the individuals, but a good idea is for each person to maintain an individual account *and* have a joint account as well for monthly expenses such as food and bills. If both partners work, their contributions to the joint account should be based on a fair percentage of their wage. You get these percentages by dividing each individual's income by the couple's total income. In money, like in marriage, there should be no secrets, no pride, and no low interest rates! To make your marriage and money last, keep communication open about your financial situation and discuss any and all large purchases.

5. I noticed a bank error on my statement in my favor. Do I get to keep the money?

Though it may seem like a gift from a higher power that you received this money, you must remember that it is not yours and you are not entitled to it. Chances are the bank will discover the error and take it back. If you have spent this money, you are liable to pay it back, and if you neglect to do so your credit will suffer— Not to mention if the money is taken out after you have spent it, it could leave your account in the negative zone and you will be responsible for the overdraft charges. If you explain the mistake and return the money, you will feel good about being honest and maybe even receive a small gift of appreciation from the bank.

6. Can I get my overdraft fees waived?

It is possible to get your overdraft fees waived by your bank, but keep in mind you are lucky if this happens. The key is to make them feel sorry for you, which shouldn't be a problem if the overdraft really wasn't your fault. Let's say your employer was late depositing your paycheck and your rent was paid that day. Go to your bank and sit down with an account representative (Avoid the tellers.), explain to them that you know it is *your fault* about the fees, but say you were shocked at the overdraft rates. The bank has every right to charge you, so ask them if there is anything you can do to avoid or at least reduce the charges. Add how loyal and responsible a customer you've been (assuming you have been) and that you would like to continue to be such a customer. Afterward, send them a nice letter praising them. Again, the bank wants you as a customer, so they just might help you out, but do *not* go in the bank angry, expecting to have people bend over backward to help you.

Thank You

Putting this book together was no easy task. With a lot of time, effort and patience I've been able to create something I am very proud of and that I think can help a lot of people.

Collaborating with my writer Dale Anderson has made this process much easier. His hard work and dedication to this project is invaluable, and I want to thank him personally for the work he's put into this book. Dale's research has added so much to the overall quality of the book and I appreciate his contributions.

Dale Anderson is a graduate from the University of Calgary and holds a Bachelor of Arts degree in English. With five years of writing and research experience, Dale's responsibilities include writing internal publications, press releases and Web site information. Dale is also Head of Customer Relations within Canam Credit Company responding to client inquiries, loan processing and stock financing.

Born and raised in Calgary, Alberta, Dale enjoys spending time with friends, working out at the gym, cooking, and participating in volunteer work.

I'd like to once again thank Dale for his hard work.

James T. White

I'd like to thank my late mother Shirley, who taught me that the darker the cloud, the brighter the silver lining. Thanks for always believing in me.

Dale Anderson

About the Author

As the founder, President, and C.E.O. of six highly successful companies, James T. White is no ordinary 22 year old. He has been building businesses for over ten years, beginning his first landscaping business at the age of 12. Armed with a $20 shovel, that venture has since expanded into a multi-million dollar corporate structure. James is the President and CEO of J & W Corporate, which encompasses his five companies: J&W Mechanical Fleet Services, J & W Lawn Care and Snow Removal, J & W Tire Trax Inc., J & W Courier and Delivery Service, and J & W Property and Asset Management. His sixth business, Canam Credit Company, Inc. is one of the most expansive and technologically advanced private lending businesses in the world.

Born and raised in Calgary, Alberta, Canada, JAMES T. WHITE is creating interest everywhere he goes. Aggressive but friendly, his confidence and ability to seize opportunities make him a corporate force. At the helm of his own successful private lending business, James is dedicated to helping other people achieve the same financial success he has seen at such a young age. His ability to bridge the gap between the millionaire business executive and the average blue-collar worker is grabbing the attention of thousands of people around North America.

Printed in the United States
77702LV00004B/1-339